THE THREE GOOD FRIDAYS

Memories of an Irish Octogenarian

WILLIAM MORRISON

authorHOUSE®

AuthorHouse™ UK
1663 Liberty Drive
Bloomington, IN 47403 USA
www.authorhouse.co.uk
Phone: UK TFN: 0800 0148641 (Toll Free inside the UK)
UK Local: 02036 956322 (+44 20 3695 6322 from outside the UK)

Published by AuthorHouse 11/18/2020

ISBN: 978-1-6655-8209-4 (sc)
ISBN: 978-1-6655-8210-0 (hc)
ISBN: 978-1-6655-8208-7 (e)

Print information available on the last page.

MORRISON

CONTENTS

ACKNOWLEDGEMENTS

Thanks to my parents, Tom and Margaret, and my sisters, Mary and Jane, for being the family who made me the person I am.

Thanks to all my friends for fully accepting Mona as honorary Irish and to Mona's family in Trinidad for equally accepting me into theirs.

Thanks to my nephew Seán Walsh for relating the "who's Mona" incident, which sparked the latent idea of recalling some memories into action.

Thanks to another nephew Kieran Walsh, who provided invaluable IT advice and assistance, without which this wee scéal would not have seen the light of day.

Thanks to Bill Hern, who most generously volunteered the Mona chapter.

Thanks to Hera Bennett, my support liaison contact at AuthorHouse UK, and the many in-house colleagues who helped along the way. Not forgetting her colleague Ned, who kept at me to act on my initial approach, which was merely for information.

With apologies to the many friends and family who have shared so many moments and experiences that could/ should have been included but unfortunately didn't make the cut! Míle Buíochas to all.

Chapter 1

WHERE IT ALL BEGAN.

I was born 10 April 1936 in Dublin, on a Good Friday and a significant day for me. Another significant Good Friday occurred on 10 April 1998, when the Northern Ireland Peace Agreement was signed in Belfast, bringing to an end more than thirty years of turmoil and strife. The latest significant event was on 10 April 2020, another Good Friday, when I endured, rather than celebrated, my eighty-fourth birthday in less than splendid isolation under government direction, cocooned in my own home despite my own good health as a result of the worldwide Covid-19 pandemic. At least I didn't have to blow out eighty-four candles to a family audience—grateful for small mercies.

I grew up in the small seaside village of Blackrock, County Dublin, a few miles south of Dublin city. The 1930s and 1940s were the times of the Emergency, as the Second World War was known in neutral Ireland at the time. It was an era of ration books, gas masks, the LDF (Local Defence Force), the LSF (Local Security Force), and ARPs (Air Raid Precautions), all manned by local volunteers while doing their regular day jobs.

The North Strand bombings took place in May 1941, causing twenty-seven civilian deaths and numerous injuries, destroying twenty-five houses, and damaging over three hundred homes. I don't remember that night, but I do recall on another occasion being woken up in the middle of the night by my parents and taken out of my bed to view the searchlights of the Irish Army searching the night sky to seek out the German bombers, which allegedly strayed off course while on a bombing raid over England. I peeped out through the heavy blackout curtains, but while I could see the beams from the powerful searchlights, I saw no bombers that night, happily.

I was about five years old at the time. Most of my other memories of that period are far less grim and generally happy. In Blackrock we lived on Frascati Park, a development of about sixty three- and four-bedroomed semi-detached houses built in the 1920s and 1930s between George's and Merrion Avenues. It was bookended by two religious establishments—by a small meeting house chapel at the George's Avenue end, which we believed served a small Plymouth Brethren Congregation, and by the more imposing St Andrews Presbyterian Church at the Merrion Avenue end. There was an unusual aspect to Frascati, in that the first fifteen houses on the right-hand side of the road were in Frascati, while the corresponding houses on the left were on George's Avenue. At Number 15, the road took a sharp right-angled turn, and thereafter, the houses on both sides of the road were all on Frascati Park.

The mixed religious persuasion of this geographical setting was reflected in the residents. We had Catholics, Protestants of the Church of Ireland, Presbyterians, and other denominations. We all got on well together, being aware of and respectful of our differences. And the children probably socialized more than the adults. The wives and widows had a quite extensive informal pattern of visiting each other's house on a one-on-one schedule of evening visits. The warm friendships were long-standing but never on a first-name basis—my mother was always Mrs Morrison, never Margaret, and her friends were always Mrs Flood, never Maud, and Mrs Joyce, never Mai. And so it was with the other ladies, Lombard, Moore, McCabe, Meagher, Kirby, Hughes, O'Neill, Breathneach, and others. The families hailed from all over Ireland—north, south, east, and west—and there were very few original Dubliners among the residents. The occupations of the neighbours comprised a broad range of professions, such as civil servants, some engineers, accountants, doctors, nurses, teachers, bankers, and at least one Garda.

For transport, there were very few cars but plenty of bicycles ridden by both adults and children alike. For public transport, there were both tram and train to reach the city. The double-decker tram ran on steel tracks embedded in cobblestones and powered by overhead electric cable. Some of the older models were open air on the top deck at the front, and as kids we imagined we were on the prow of a ship with the wind and rain blowing in our faces à la the much later film *Titanic*. The last tram ceased operation in 1948—the end of romance, to be replaced by more modern buses. The trains were both local commuter and long distance, and adult commuters who worked in town— we never called it the city—availed themselves of the train to come home to lunch, as was the custom of the time. The trains were of the old steam variety, belching black coal smoke and smut and sounding the steam whistle signal.

The children, like their parents, got along well with one another despite going to different religious schools. We played road tennis, tying a rope across the road between two lamp posts as the net. For roller hockey we used hockey sticks and hurleys, making up our own rules. We also played cricket, soccer, marbles, and conkers (chestnuts) in season. There were no commercial children's camps as they currently exist, and we never missed them even if we were occasionally bored. The various associations, such as

Boy Scouts, Boys' Brigade, and Girl Guides, did conduct camping holidays. But for our main summer pastime and playground, we had the open-sea, open-air bathing pools commonly called the Baths.

10 Metre High High Diving stage, Blackrock Baths

The Blackrock Baths were originally built in the 1880s and upgraded a few times—the last in the 1950s, soon enough for our teenage enjoyment—before being closed and abandoned by the Dun Laoghaire Corporation in the late 1980s after a century in operation. The summer season ran from May through September, and the baths provided endless hours of enjoyment. We swam and dived on a daily basis from early morning to late in the evenings, with occasional breaks for lunch and dinner, at the time referred to as dinner and tea. It was a veritable crèche for teenagers. There were regular swimming, diving, and water polo competitions throughout the season.

In 1948, the Olympic Games were held in London, and the Irish Olympic team was represented by Eddie Heron in diving and Paddy Kavanagh in swimming, both members of Sandycove based at Blackrock. I too was a member of the Sandycove club, and at the age of twelve I had the privilege of rubbing shoulders with them most mornings, on the odd occasion getting tips, training, and coaching from these elite sportsmen. These interactions fostered my lifelong involvement in the sports of Diving swimming and water polo.

We attended a variety of local schools. These included Willow Park, Blackrock College, Christian Brothers Dun Laoghaire, Sion Hill, Avoca, and Alexandra College, and in the case of my two sisters, Mary and Jane, the Irish language school in Loreto Convent, St Stephen's Green in central Dublin.

I started my schooling at the tender age of four and a half years at Carysfort Convent National School run by the order of Mercy nuns. It was an Irish-language school. I have a distinct memory of a very confusing first day in a new and strange environment. I had no understanding of what was happening; nor did I grasp a word of this strange and unfamiliar language. However, I soon got to grips with the new vernacular and became so adept with it that, by the time I left at eight years old, I was so fluent in Irish that I never had to struggle with the Gaeilge for the rest of my secondary education and learned to love not only the tongue itself but also the rich culture and the opening it gave me to explore the country's history, music, and song. Thank you, Sisters Claver and Walburga. Go raibh maith agaibh! After all those years, I am still friendly with one of my classmates, Des Ellison, from that forty-pupil class of 1941, nearly eighty years ago.

Shopping was mostly carried out on the village main street, which had a selection of choices. Among them were four butchers, Graham Bros., O'Malleys, Taaffes, and Horlacher Pork Butchers. There were two chemists, Parkes and O'Neills and two dairies, Byrnes on Carysfort Avenue and Grahams on George's Avenue. McKinley Hardware dominated the scene. And the home-made ice cream from the sweet shops of the O'Byrne brothers, Leo ran Budina and Gerry the Wee-Shop, made it the target of the young folk. In addition, there was the very important cycle repair service of Mr Hempenstall. The barber was Mr de Mangeat. For general groceries and foodstuffs, we had Lipton's, Payantake, and Findlater's. A feature of the latter was the intriguing overhead pneumatic pulley paying system, which carried cash and change via containers to the elevated central cashiers desk and the service counters. This was a big attraction for the trailing kids of the shopping housewives. There were a few pubs and betting shops, but we never patronized them, being underage.

For entertainment there was the Regent Cinema, a single-storey building that had a change of programme twice weekly. Admission charges were 6 p (sixpence) for the front stalls, or woodeners as they were known; 8 p (eight pence) for the central stalls; and 1 s (one shilling) for the back stalls. I remember seeing Larry Parks in *The Jolson Story* and *Jolson Sings Again*, among many happy years of film going.

To supplement the village shops, there was a vigorous home delivery service that covered daily delivery of freshly baked bread by three different bakeries by horse-drawn vans. Milk in bottles and in loose bulk was also transported by horse-drawn traps contained in two large metal churns .The order was taken at the customer's front door on the day and measured by the pint into the housewife's own vessel. To ensure that full measure was provided, an extra drop was added and known as the "tilley".

The postman called twice a day delivering letters early morning and late afternoon.

Less frequent were the visits of the fishmonger, who wheeled his wheelbarrow each Friday, announcing his arrival by calling out loudly for all the residents to hear, "Fresh fish! Fresh fish!"

And they certainly did hear him. Once, when queried if the fish were fresh, he called out to his assistant, "Willy, will you kill a mackerel for Mrs Kelly?"

Occasionally we had a cutler visit with his two-wheeler mobile workshop, which incorporated a workbench at which he sat and sharpened the knives, scissors, hatchets and lawnmowers. He offered an unusual service, which ensured the street was at the cutting edge.

The last of our traveling vendors was really a troubadour, who filled our summer months with music. He was an ex-army trumpeter, who serenaded the street with such numbers as "Ciri Biri Bin: Oh Mein Papa," "Cherry Pink and Apple Blossom White," "Carnival of Venice," and "The Flight of the Bumble Bee". He was a busker long before it became common on Dublin's Grafton Street in recent times.

In contrast, the other sound we regularly heard, usually on Saturday mornings, was the all-clear air raid siren, which was held as a practice exercise and was a reassuring sound if not very melodious. Happily, it wasn't used in real-life war conditions in neutral Ireland, to our good fortune.

Finally, there were two major seasonal fuel deliveries, which occurred in the autumn, with coal and wood deliveries of ton loads or half ton or quarter ton lots from the coal and timber fuel merchants. In those days, we had no central heating in the homes, just open fireplaces.

A neighbour of ours had an allotment in the nearby Dublin mountains, where he harvested his winters supply of turf, and we sometimes joined in on the turf cutting. It was invigorating work and usually came with an attack of midges, which left us scratching for all the following week. But we were rewarded with a complimentary supply of turf for our efforts.

CHAPTER 2

HAPPY SCHOOL YEARS

From 1944 to 1954, I spent ten very happy years at Willow Park Primary School and Blackrock College Secondary School under the care of the Holy Ghost Order. We had a first-class education, where we learnt the lessons of life not only in the classrooms but also on the playing fields of the campus. The curriculum covered the conventional subjects but also included options for music, drama, art, and elocution and debating. On the sporting side of things, we played rugby, cricket, tennis, as well as the lesser sports of handball and table tennis. In the summer term athletics was our main occupation.

Rugby was our strongest sport in terms of inter-schools competitions, and many of the pupils went on as senior players to represent the province (Leinster) and the Irish national team. One Niall Brophy played for the Four Nations Lions touring team.

The lessons learned on the playing pitches combined with the academic lessons ensured a spirit of discipline, justice, courage, and generosity to our fellow classmates and society in general. The school motto was "Fides et Robur" (Faith and Strength).

The friendships formed at school endured all my life. We had day boys and boarders from all over the country. The Holy Ghost Order being a missionary order, we had pupils from Britain and the Americas, mostly the sons of Irish emigrants. Those from farther afield came from those countries where there were Holy Ghost colleges and houses—the continent of Africa, Asia's Hong Kong, Singapore, and Malaya (now renamed Malayasia). Two boys I particularly remember were twin brothers, Chin en Qui and Chin en Ko, known as Richard and Roland Chin. They were called "The Double Chins".

I was a mediocre rugby player, never getting on the school team. But that didn't matter. Enjoying the fun of the game was what was important. The ambition was to win, but to learn to lose graciously was equally important. And I did learn to do so frequently.

I did make the cricket eleven up till the age of fourteen, when my love of the water took over. And Blackrock Baths were my playground for the next few years. I was captain of the school swimming club. We won the school water polo titles and various individual and team swimming championships, and I won springboard and high-diving titles.

Sports day was the big occasion for our athletes, and the leading athletes revelled in the various running and field event competitions. For the non-elite athletes, however, the highlight of the day was the slow bicycle race, the winner of which was the one who crossed the finish line of the hundred-yard track last—or was the last remaining upright cyclist, all the others having fallen off their bikes in trying to go too slowly. The specialists in this technique were the Ellison brothers, perennial winners of the event.

CHAPTER 3

AN ORDINARY FAMILY

Standing: Father & Author
Front row: Sister Mary, Mother, Sister Jane.
Early 1950's

Growing up, my two sisters, Mary and Jane, and I assumed

we were part of an ordinary family. Looking back in later

life, we were still of the same opinion. However, we did agree there were aspects of our family life that were far from ordinary. And those related to the unusual characteristics of our parents.

My father, Tom Morrison, came from a small village, Ballysimon, a few miles outside Limerick City. And my mother, Margaret Rafferty, was from about twenty miles down the road from Monard, an equally small town land near Limerick Junction and a similar distance from Tipperary Town. On marriage, they both moved to Dublin, where my father became a civil servant in the Customs and Excise Service, and my mother graduated as a nurse in the Saint Vincent's Hospital, then based in Stephen's Green.

My father had enjoyed an active sporting career in Limerick, captaining his senior school's hurling team to victory in the Munster Schools Harty Cup. He was also an Irish step dancing champion as a teenager and an adult— long before *Riverdance*! In the 1924 and 1928 traditional national Tailteann Games, he was an All-Ireland Tailteann champion, winning two gold medals and a bronze medal in the reel, hornpipe, and jig classes.

Consequently, he was offered a part in the John McCormack Hollywood film by the Fox Corporation *Peg O' My Heart*. However, the gamble of a speculative film career on the basis of just one film versus the security of his permanent civil service job proved too much. So he stuck to the day job, and we never grew up as Hollywood brats—to our undying disappointment!

As an adult in Dublin, my father played rugby and, at a later stage, golf on a weekly basis. He also maintained an active interest as a spectator in the Gaelic sports of hurling and Gaelic football and took me to games, particularly in Croke Park, the main stadium of the Gaelic Athletic Association. I remember being on Hill Sixteen when it was grass surfaced.

My parents were a team and gave us a very balanced upbringing. We had a small suburban back garden, and they planted and grew potatoes, cabbages, peas, lettuce, strawberries, and asparagus, which gave us an appreciation and education of the value of nutrition and where our food came from.

On winter nights sitting around the coal fire, our father would read us chapters of the classics. Sir Walter Scott's *Ivanhoe* still sticks in my mind seventy odd years later.

Other aspects of their positive parenting include that we were sent to art classes, well drawing and painting, and also got piano lessons till we proved ourselves as not being talented enough to benefit from them.

Mother, as was obligatory at the time, retired from nursing on marriage and devoted herself to full-time homemaking and all its domestic chores. Despite her full-time housekeeping, she also found time to engage in leather work. And with no formal training, she made pampooties, gloves, and slippers, which she sold through leading city stores, such as Arnotts and Switzer's. She also designed and made ladies' fashion hats, which she also negotiated for sale successfully on a part-time basis. It was years later that we children, as adults, discovered that not everybody's mother did likewise. Not bad for a farmer's daughter.

Years later, when my father died at fifty-four years of age, she was a young widow and resumed her nursing activities on a private basis, mainly caring for neighbours with minor ailments and the odd injection as directed by the family doctors of the area. Sometimes, she would convey the patients to the doctor or hospital. And to be strictly within the law, she acquired a commercial hackney licence to carry passengers for hire. As a backup, I too qualified for the commercial hackney licence, which I was very infrequently called on to employ. As an active elderly seventy-year-old, she used to help out with the local voluntary "old folks" society.

CHAPTER 4

THE ADULT YEARS: WORK AND PLAY

On leaving school at eighteen, my ambition was to become a pilot. The way to do so was to enlist in the Irish Army Air Corps; serve for a fixed term; and then transfer to Aer Lingus, the national commercial airline. It was not to be, however, as, on presenting myself for the medical test, to my surprise, I failed the optical test; I was diagnosed as colour blind—a fact of which I was completely unaware. This was one of my first big lessons in how to deal with and overcome disappointments and not feel sorry for myself.

So for the next ten years I worked in a number of different jobs and companies, all the while gaining experience and skills that stayed with me throughout my entire working life. The companies I worked with included:

- M Duan & Company—waste paper merchants
- Irish Dunlop Rubber Company—motor transport / cycle tyres and tennis and golf equipment
- Remington Rand International—office equipment and computers
- Érin Foods Semi-State Food Enterprise—freeze-dried agricultural products, domestic and export
- Bord Fáilte—Irish government tourist board, domestic and international

Duan collected waste paper from the city offices, factories, and private homes with a fleet of a half dozen trucks and vans. It was then sorted, graded, and bailed to be sold to a number of major paper mills for recycling into fresh paper of different standards, by a workforce of over one hundred girls and women from the local community. They sat around large sorting tables about ten to a table sorting and singing the local pop tunes all day long, in many cases substituting in their own words with local references to spice up the songs. It made for a very interesting and culturally enlightening education. It was recycling and the green ethos long before it became the common mantra of today.

From there, I moved on to Dunlop, where I gained wide experience with an international organization in general commercial and administrative practices. This involved customer service weeks around the country in the motor trade, motor trialling, and scrambling competitions and also the amateur cycling domestic and international field.

Jobs were hard to find and equally hard to hold on to. However, I was keen to progress and got to the stage I needed a change of scene. But it took me over two hundred applications to advertisements and twenty interviews before I succeeded—such was the tight job market in the early sixties. Three hard sales years in Remington Rand on basic salary and commission honed my sales and marketing skills, which enabled me to join the newly developing Érin Foods state commercial enterprise in 1963.

We launched a range of Irish agricultural products processed by a new freeze-dried technique and marketed to the catering and hospitality trade nationally and, shortly after, in Britain. As part of the pioneer sales force, I spent a year in the North of England based in Manchester for what originally was meant to be a three-month launch period. But such was our success that, to keep up with the business, I was persuaded to stay on. My first taste of voluntary emigration, happily, was painless, unlike the experience of many of my fellow Irish emigrants who were forced by economic conditions to leave Ireland involuntarily. I encountered lots of national differences. For example, when going into a bakery to buy bread, I asked for a loaf—a sliced pan as we called it in Ireland. The puzzled response I got from the shop girl was "Sorry, luv! This is a bakery, not a hardware shop!"

And so, in 1965 a colleague pointed out an ad for a sales and marketing executive in the newly established marketing arm of Bord Fáilte –the national government tourist board and persuaded me to apply, which I did with no great expectations but completely fancy free. To my surprise and almost consternation, I was successful. So I had a big decision to make. I did and never regretted it, for the next thirty-five very fulfilled years.

CHAPTER 5

BORD FÁILTE HIGHLIGHTS

A few of the highlights during my years at the Irish tourist board include:

- *1969 (17 March).* Saint Patrick's Day Parade— first US college marching band visit
- *1972 (July).* Muhammad Ali versus Al " Blue" Lewis in Croke Park, GAA HQ
- *1979.* John Paul Papal visit—one and a quarter million at Phoenix Park papal Mass
- *1993.* Golden Oldies International Rugby Festival—4,500+ participants up to eighty years old

- *1994/1995.* Eurovision International Song Contest Dublin—*Riverdance* launch
- *1995 (1 December).* United States President Bill Clinton visit to Dublin
- *1998.* Tour de France—three-day start in Ireland
- *2011 (23 May).* United States President Barack O'Bama (Obama), Dublin

My time at the Irish Tourist Board, Bord Fáilte, involved working with the tourist and hospitality industry worldwide to encourage existing and future expansion of visitor traffic to Ireland. We worked in conjunction with international airlines, shipping and cruise lines, travel agents, and tour operators, as well as with international media, television, radio, and print outlets. In our day-to-day operations, we worked closely with all the elements of the Irish tourist and leisure industry, with their willing cooperation, providing them with all the tools to enhance their individual and collective profitable businesses.

There was tremendous job satisfaction, knowing that we were contributing to the national economic well-being of the nation and also to the prosperity and happiness of the individual members of the Irish tourist and cultural communities. I'm happy to say that every day was a great day to get to go to work and was always full of challenge. There are so many examples of the joys of the job, which became almost a vocation, that some examples seem worth the telling. It's not so much the big events that linger as much as some of the more intimate moments that bring a smile.

To brighten up our annual Saint Patrick's Day observations, which in the sixties were quite low-key, we invited the students of the Irish Christian Brothers Bishop Kearney High School Band, based in America to visit the home of their founder Edmund Ignatious Rice in the village of Callan County Carlow. They came for a week and were the highlight of the Dublin parade. It was the first time an American college marching band appeared, and they were an immediate success. Their reception in Callan was even more sensational and a mutually warm experience for both the locals and visitors. The visit was, in deed, so successful that, for every 17 March since, Saint Patrick's Day parades throughout Ireland have featured lots of visiting bands, not only from North America but also from numerous other countries, adding a truly international and colourful flavour to our national celebrations.

Muhammad Ali

His first visit to Ireland was to fight Al " Blue " Lewis in a non title bout which took place in the open air at Croke Park Dublin, I attended that fight in a working capacity.

A few years after the Muhammad Ali fight in Dublin's Croke Park, I encountered him in New York's Madison Garden after a fight night at which we were both spectators. I had the good fortune to have an engaging conversation with him, and in the banter, we discussed his Irish visit and experience. He was very affable and gracious and made brief reference to his ancient Irish heritage connection.

I first saw him fight in 1960 at the Olympics in Rome, where he fought as an amateur on the US boxing team as Cassius Clay and won the light heavyweight title and Olympic medal. On his return to America, he subsequently threw away his medal in the course of converting to the black Muslim religion. Happily when we met and had our chat later in New York, he had mellowed a lot. And our interaction left me with warm memories.

The Papal Visit

The papal visit of Pope John Paul was announced a mere six weeks before his arrival, and the announcement created a scurry of activity in religious and civil circles. It was a short time to prepare for this first ever papal visit—one that would unite those of all faiths and none in a multiplicity of coordinated committees—and to ensure a smooth event. The highlight of the visit was a papal mass in the phoenix park at which one and a quarter million were in attendance.

"Golden Oldies" Rugby

By contrast the following year, a rugby festival for "Golden Oldies"—those age thirty-five and up—attracted over 4,500 players of various conditions of fitness to a week-long jamboree. Teams were graded by age—over thirty-five, over forty-five, and so on, with rules modified as the age category increased. The oldest team competitor was age eighty years plus from Japan; he only stayed on the pitch for about five minutes and got one touch of the rugby ball before retiring unscathed.

Eurovision Song Contest

On a promotional trip to Malta, I was approached by a local travel agent to help him secure tickets for the Eurovision Song Contest. The contest was being held in Dublin as a result of Niamh Kavanagh winning the event the previous year, and this was Malta's first time securing entry to the competition. Unfortunately, all tickets were sold out.

When Ireland won the second year in a row—and would thus be hosting the next year—I made a deal to supply the tickets for Malta and for other potential music fans. As a result, we attracted over three hundred enthusiasts from an entirely new source of interest.

When, a few years later, Ireland won again, we were able to tap this specialty market to attract another several hundred Eurovision fans. At the interval, a seven-minute Irish music and dance performance entranced the international audience and became the act that subsequently enchanted audiences globally as *Riverdance*, the show.

Demand for tickets was very high, and my authority to control them was strictly regulated—they were to be available only to overseas visitors. I was inundated with requests from local sources, which I had to refuse, including some requests from employees of our co-sponsors Telefís Éireann, the national television service. One female employee from RTÉ was particularly insistent, but I was equally insistent in having to refuse her on the grounds of our international allocation rules.

When the show became the fantastic worldwide sensation it soon was, imagine my mixed emotions when that woman turned out to be Moya Doherty, the co-producer of *Riverdance*! She had been the producer of the original seven-minute interval act that had become the international *Riverdance* sensation.

President Clinton

President Clinton's visit as part of his support of the peace negotiations in Northern Ireland gave a boost to tourism in the Republic. And as part of the welcoming organizing committee I was happy to receive a letter of thanks from the White House for the welcoming arrangements. The Belfast Good Friday agreement was signed on 10 April 1998.

Tour de France

The Tour de France started off the mainland of Europe for the first time when, in three days in July '98, Ireland was the centre of attention of the world's most important professional event, commanding one of the world's most extensive sporting television audiences. Such coverage also proved valuable in general tourism coverage. Working with the French tour organizers was an interesting and enjoyable campaign, covering twelve month's preparation and execution.

In summer 2019, a French movie concerning the tour was made, partially in Dublin. I had the pleasurable experience of reliving some of the memories of the original tour; meeting up with some of those involved in the 1972 event and also, for fun, taking part as a voluntary cast extra. C'était si bon!

O'Bama

The public address of president O'Bama's (Obama's) visit to the Irish public took place on Dublin's Dame Street. I was witness to a charming incident—an interaction between the president and a local teenage girl as he was on his way to the podium to address the crowd. She was on her mobile phone as he passed and stopped to shake spectators outstretched hands .The girl seized the moment to thrust her mobile into his hands with the directive, "Speak to my mother."

In the relaxed spirit of the occasion, he gladly did so. After holding a brief conversation with the absent girl's mother, he handed back the phone; mounted the podium' and gave a polished public address, including his famous Irish language translation of the "Is Féidir Linn" (Yes, we can) mantra.

Working Overseas

In the course of these working years, I spent a number of years based overseas. On two occasions, I was in North America as a sales and market development manager, and in between, I worked as sales manager in Britain. All provided interesting and contrasting experiences.

Britain in the early seventies was a difficult assignment, as the Northern Ireland political scene was in an uneasy state, making it difficult to persuade potential tourists that all was calm and welcoming in the Republic. However, I never encountered any personal animosity from the general public. I encountered the same perceptions in North America. But an Irish accent was never a disadvantage in the new world.

There were culture shocks in both exiles, both good and bad. On my appointment as sales manager, on arrival in New York, I was interviewed by journalist broadcaster Sally Jessy Raphael. She said, "You are going to love New York, and you are going to hate New York." My experiences proved her correct, but there was more of the love and less of the hate.

Social Life and The Performing Arts

Throughout my career, my social life was not neglected. After all, "All work and no play make Jack a dull boy." So I continued competitive swimming and diving, representing the Irish universities in the World Student Games in Sofia, Bulgaria, in 1961. Another member of that team was our great hero Ronnie Delany, the 1956 Melbourne Olympics champion, who of course won the 800-metre title. At home, we took part in national championships. We also gave serious attention to comedy trick-diving exhibitions— featuring sailing off the ten-metre diving boards on bicycles, off step ladders, on stilts, and through flaming hoops, some of them in drag and all for fun!

Dublin life was full of theatre, both classical and traditional, at The Abbey Theatre; cinema; and music of many genres. Both Irish and international performers entertained us. We knew we were the centre of the world, even if we were living on an island, off another island and obviously, so too did the cast of international singers and musicians who regularly visited to receive warm welcomes

Performers at the 3,500-seat Royal Theatre ranged from Danny Kaye and Billy Eckstein to Lena Horn, Nat King Cole, and Guy Mitchell at different times and in different years. The Carlton featured Bill Haley and his Comets and Glen Campbell, also in different years. At the Adelphi, Ella Fitzgerald and Oscar Peterson were the stars. And the Olympia hosted Kris Kristofferson and Emmy Lou Harris on several visits. In more recent times, Tony Bennett and Al Martino became repeat performers at the National Concert Hall and were welcomed as two of our own. We also had big outdoor concerts with the Everly Brothers, Simon and Garfunkel, and Paul McCartney, all of whose concerts and performances I attended over the years. I enjoyed these performers, together with a host of native performers, not all of whom were internationally known but were superb entertainers nevertheless.

Ulysses the Movie

In summer 1967, Joe Strick, the Broadway producer, came to Ireland to film the James Joyce classic *Ulysses* in the Dublin locale. Here the masterpiece, describing the entire happenings of one day, 16 June, takes place.

On the first day of filming, I got a frantic call to my office from the logistics manager of the company. They were in urgent need of a stand-in for the opening scene as a result of an incident involving their leading man. The film opened in the Forty Foot bathing place with the actor T P McKenna plunging naked into the "scrotum-tightening snot-green sea" in the words of the author. However, disdaining the use of a body double, T P proved to be a better actor than aquatic performer, as he executed a belly-flopper and really tightened his scrotum! A replacement was required urgently in order not to delay the production. I was happy to respond, hopped out of the office, and spent a very interesting day working in the movies.

With lots of retakes, I was completely exhausted by the end of shooting for the day.

41

I also performed for Molly Bloom's "yes, yes, yes" sequence.

The matter of payment was intriguing. As an amateur sportsman, I was subject to the competition rules, which were quite strict in those days. So I was paid for my artistic and cultural input, rather than for my diving expertise.

As the book and film operated under censorship restrictions, it was almost thirty years before the film enjoyed a public commercial performance in Dublin. However, on completion of filming, Strick hired a commercial cinema, The Corinthian, in central Dublin for a private premier showing and invited all those involved in the production—actors, technicians, and yours truly to a midnight matinee. It was a generous gesture of thanks to all the Irish participants.

That concluded my illustrious movie career.

***

My interest in music was more than adequately catered for in the course of my postings across the Atlantic in the late sixties and mid seventies. My friend Ronnie Kavanagh said to me, on hearing of my official job description as sales manager, North America, "They didn't stint you for territory!"

The change of location was a huge culture shock. But after a short while, as the big brash New York City became more familiar, it began to feel more like Manhattan village. Little encounters eased our homesickness. A smattering included seeing Gene Kelly skipping and dancing across a Broadway street, passing by Rod McKuen in his jeans and runners, and not recognizing the innocuous couple walking towards us on the sidewalk till I recognized the distinctive voice of the actress Joanne Woodward and her handsome companion Paul Newman and the friendly response to our surprised salute. Then it began to feel like home.

In 1968, the musical *Hair* was reflective of the West Coast flower power children of San Francisco and featured such numbers as "Aquarius/Let the Sunshine in" and Good Morning Sunshine". It opened on Broadway with a mixed cast, including the beautiful Marsha Hunt, she of the Black Power poster "Black is Beautiful" that adorned bedroom walls on both sides of the Atlantic at that time. Marsha

Hunt later moved to Ireland for a while and taught drama to Mountjoy prisoners as a public service.

A number of musicals featured all Afro American cast members—who, at that stage were known as "black," having earlier been designated "coloured" and then "negro" (all of which was a wee bit confusing to a red-headed freckled Irishman trying to be politically correct through the decades). Pearl Bailey starred in a black *Hello, Dolly!* Melba Moore was the lead in *Pearlie*, a story about a preacher's return to the Deep South. I attended a matinee performance where I was the only white member of the audience, which was a thrilling experience, as audience participation was so wholehearted that there were as many *hallelujahs* and *amens* emanating from the stalls as from the stage. Another ethnic musical was *Fiddler on the Roof*, starring Topol in the main role.

On the cabaret scene, Shirley Bassey was a regular—before she became a dame. And Eubie Blake and his " Love Will Find a Way"—the pixie-like pianist enthralling his audience in the New York Town Hall—remains in my memory at ninety-three years of age.

On Saint Patrick's Day, 17 March, the musical scene turned green. And Carnegie Hall was the venue for an Irish ceilidh, featuring the likes of the Clancy Brothers and Tommy Makem; The Chieftains; John Gary; and the Afro American singer Maxine Sullivan, a contemporary of Ella Fitzgerald who was very proud of her Irish heritage.

Mention of Carnegie Hall brings to mind the hoary old joke, "How do you get to Carnegie Hall?"

"Practice! Practice! Practice!"

On 24 May 1974, the death of Edward K. (Duke) Ellington at the age of seventy-five was announced. And the public in Manhattan was invited to pay their respects at the funeral home, where his body lay in open casket for several days. It was an opportunity not to be missed, and so my wife, Mona Baptiste, a singer in her own right, and I accepted the invitation and paid our respects. We also attended the funeral service in Harlem's Saint John, the divine Episcopalian cathedral, some days later. The requiem was a very moving ceremony, with three priests celebrating the high Mass. The congregation was composed of the plain people of Harlem, as well as the who's who of the American jazz scene, who'd flown in from all around the country to pay tribute and participate in the ceremonies.

As Catholics, we found the Episcopalian service familiar and quite similar to ours. But this was not the case for all the mourners. A fellow pew member remarked in relation to the sweet-smelling incense in the thurible, "Hey dig the cool cat with the crazy grass."

Mahalia Jackson sang the Lord's Prayer, and Joe Jones, one of the leading drummers of his generation, broke a national tour to attend from Philadelphia. It was a most inspiring occasion, especially when the entire five thousand-strong mixed attendees joined together to sing the final hymns in truly ecumenical harmony.

In contrast, on the West Coast, I was fortunate to get to see three of the Mills Brothers perform and give us their smooth renderings of their favourites, "Glowworm," "Paper Doll," and others. I was also introduced to Turk Murphy, he of the *San Francisco Jazz Band*, famous for, among others, his hit " Night Train". It was quite a thrill to be socializing with a musician whose records I had listened to back home in Ireland where he was a well-known name.

The Las Vegas (Irish) Outpost

Joe Delaney was an Irish American lawyer, record producer, theatre critic, and documentary maker living in Las Vegas. He was also a very good friend to Ireland and the various Irish musicians and entertainers who visited and passed through over the years, including the Irish showband cabarets. He was especially supportive of Irish tourism interests and became a fond friend of mine in my stateside years. He organized the Saint Patrick's Day Parade and conducted the annual Rose of Tralee Festival selection ball. He became known as the Irish doorman, as he made so many helpful introductions and opened so many doors for visiting Irish entertainers.

On the social side, he also introduced my wife, Mona, and me to many celebrities. To chat with the likes of Tony Bennett, Bob Newhart, and Joanie Rivers was quite an experience, particularly as I was introduced as the overall head of the Irish government's tourist bureau, a slight exaggeration and a flattering promotion. We viewed one of his documentaries on Ireland in Paul Anka's home studio and shared an elevator with Kirk Douglas in immaculate whites on his way to the tennis courts. But the intro that remains vividly in view of more recent revelations was our warm and entertaining encounter and banter with the now discredited Bill Cosby, who was at the height of his popularity at the time. History takes funny turns.

CHAPTER 6

MORE FAMILY

**Fr. Michael Morrison ministering to the dead at
mass grave with fellow army chaplain at Bergen
Belsen concentration camp** (Date 1945)

My father's youngest brother, Michael, on his ordination as a Jesuit priest in late 1939, accepted an invitation from his superior to answer a call for chaplains to join the British Army. Initially, he served in Egypt with the Eighth Army desert campaign. Subsequently, with the 11th Armoured Division, he was with the troops who entered and liberated Bergen-Belsen Concentration Camp. The experience had a lasting effect on him for the rest of his life.

The following is a copy of a letter he wrote to one of his sisters, Nora in the early days of his duties.

My Dearest Nor,

I am in Belsen Concentration Camp. There has been quite a lot about it recently on the BBC. It has been very thoroughly filmed and photographed, but I expect the photos would not be published in Irish papers. I have seen some of the photos which appeared in English papers, but they do not reproduce anything like the real horror of this place. When we got here there were some thousands of naked dead bodies lying about the place. In one pile alone there were over a thousand women's bodies and it was quite common to see people crawl on their hands and knees because they were too weak to walk, while others just dropped to the ground and remained there. There were sixty thousand people crowded into an area of much less than a mile square. Some of the huts in which they lived had bunks. It was not uncommon to find three people in one bunk—one or more of whom were dead. Huts which could accommodate thirty were made to hold five to seven hundred.

So far I have buried over fifteen thousand and I have not been able to attend all funerals, as I considered the dying more important than the dead.

Your affectionate brother,
Mick

As children, we were not exposed to the horrors Uncle Mick endured. But in later life as adults, we became aware of them, though we never discussed them in depth with him.

On the sixtieth anniversary of the liberation of Belsen, Belvedere College, where he had served his last days, put on a ceremony by the students in honour of my Uncle Mick and as an educational exercise for the younger generation, who would have had little knowledge of the horrors of war. Three of the four survivors of Belsen then living in Ireland took part. One of them, Tomi Reichental, now speaks to schools and communities, not in anger but just so the atrocities will not be forgotten or repeated. He has written a book, *I Was a Boy in Belsen*, in which he mentioned Fr. Michael S J in appreciation. Tomi and I have stayed in touch and he asked me to read the letter in a documentary on his Belsen experience. We are the same age, and I count myself very lucky to have been kicking football in school in Ireland at nine years of age while, in his own words, Tomi was playing around the dead corpses, knowing no better at the same time. He's an extraordinary hero, with no bitterness.

I have been honoured to partake in the annual National Holocaust Memorial ceremony on more than one occasion as a result.

At the other end of the family age spectrum was one of my grand-nephews Donal Walsh (of *Donal Walsh—My Story*), who died of cancer at sixteen years of age. Donal had an extraordinary emotional effect on me—as he did on the entire country, following an appearance on national television on Brendan O'Connor's show, recounting his medical struggles and positive philosophy regarding his impending death. For four years, he was under treatment— with two recoveries and, finally, three relapses.

Donal was a keen sports fanatic, especially for rugby. And when he was no longer fit enough to play, he took over the training of his own peers' team—a fourteen-year-old trainer of his under-fourteen fellow students' team. The local senior Gaelic football and rugby teams took him under their wings, and he ended up attending the training sessions of the Munster and Irish rugby international teams. Paul O'Connell the Irish captain referred to him as his friend and introduced him to his fellow international teammates, two of whom in particular showed him much kindness. Shane Jennings of Leinster and Rory Best of Ulster presented him with an Ulster jersey.

Denis O'Brien, the much-maligned businessman, was also very supportive in a discreet way. When Donal was diagnosed and told that his cancer was terminal, he instated a campaign to encourage teenagers with problems to seek help rather than to seek relief in suicide, stressing that there was help available, whereas Donal had no choice as his fate was sealed. His message was reported by the county coroner to have reduced the incidence of suicide after his television appearance.

Days before his death on 12 May 2013, he was surrounded by his family. Waking up from sleep seeing the family around the bed, his humour still came through when he whispered, "Hey, lads, this is like a scene from *The Sopranos!*"

His cheeky memory still lives on.

Donnal Walsh (1996-3013)

CHAPTER 7

AND YET MORE FAMILY: WHO IS MONA?

In the late sixties, I was on a week-long international tourism promotional visit to Baden-Baden in Germany, which concluded with a spectacular gala ball on the last night. I was introduced to the solo artist Mona Baptiste, who was filming that week and also headlining the closing night concert.

At the end of the week, we went our separate ways— me back to Ireland and she back to Munich, where she'd been resident for many years. A few years later, while I was based in London, we met up again briefly as she was passing through on her way home to Trinidad, where she was born, for a family reunion. After that, we corresponded sporadically long distance and got married in Munich, on the basis that we could save on postage stamps in a more enjoyable fashion.

We both continued our respective careers, and within two weeks of our Irish honeymoon, she was back on stage in concert on the continent. As we were both well used to travel in our work, the frequent separations were taken in our stride and were a comfortable arrangement throughout our happy marriage, which lasted twenty-two years, till her death in 1973.

Mona was born in Trinidad, of Anglo Indian and Carib heritage, and had her own weekly programme on Radio Trinidad at the age of thirteen. She moved to Britain on the *Empire Windrush*, when Caribbean emigrants were welcomed as part of the family of the empire. Her singing career took off shortly after arrival, and she performed on stage and in cabaret and on radio with the BBC. She teamed up with Stéphane Grapelli, musical partner of Django Reinhardt of the Hot Club de France.

Over the years, she sang in English, French, and Spanish, and as a result, her work spread to the continent. She eventually moved to Germany, where we met. She recorded a number of hits in English and German, in addition to her public performances. While based in Ireland and always happy to introduce herself as Mona Morrison, she still continued to commute to Europe for her gigs and appeared in radio and television with among others on separate stations, Bing Crosby and Al Martino, under her professional name of Baptiste. She did, however, manage to appear on local Irish Telefís Éireann in a Maeve Binchy play, *Dearly Departed*, in an acting role.

Who is Mona?

In recent years, more than twenty years after her death, a nephew of mine, Seán Walsh, was undergoing medical treatment. He had a family team of three voluntary carers, his daughter, Lesley, a niece, and a friend, all just twenty years of age. In recounting some family history to them one day. he mentioned a painting of a restaurant Mona and I had given him as a wedding present and explained that the restaurant was where Mona used to go for coffee. He was met with blank stares and a question: "Who's Mona?" They had been born around the same time of her death, and one added, "We always thought he was a confirmed self-satisfied bachelor!"

Time had passed sufficiently for their innocent ignorance to be amusing to Seán, myself, and the older members of the family.

It was an illustration that history is seen through a different perspective by different generations. And it got me thinking that I'd better set the record straight before it's too late! It also got me thinking of the changes I've seen over the years, as well as the changes my country has undergone in my lifetime.

CHAPTER 8

CONTRIBUTION BY AUTHOR BILL HERN

Liam and I became friends when I was researching the life of his wife, the wonderful, multitalented Mona Baptiste-Morrison. I will one day publish a 200-page book about Mona, but in the meantime Liam has asked me to encapsulate Mona's life and their relationship in a page or two. I will try!

When Liam told me the "who's Mona" story recounted later in these pages, I was horrified at the thought that the younger members of his family were unaware of his marriage to Mona. It is akin to the family of Richard

Burton not knowing he was once (or, rather, twice) married to Elizabeth Taylor.

So let me introduce those younger Walshes to the lady who would have been their Aunt Mona.

When shown a photograph of Mona, everyone—male and female—first comments on her beauty. Yes, nieces and nephews, your Uncle Liam was married to one of the most beautiful women of her day.

To be fair to Liam, he wasn't punching all that much above his weight. When he met Mona in the late 1960s, he was young, fit, good-looking, athletic, intelligent, and travelling the world in a high-powered job. It was a marriage of equals, although it is more than fair to say that Mona's singing voice and acting talents far exceeded those of her husband.

There are other things that might surprise the younger Walshes. For example, Mona was black. No big deal in the twenty-first century, perhaps, but mixed marriages were still illegal in parts of the United States as recently as June 1967.

Mona and Liam married in Munich in 1972 and then settled in Dublin shortly afterwards. It won't have been solely because of their glamorous good looks that the citizens of that fair city stopped to take a second glance at this couple. A black face in Dublin was still a rarity.

Mona was born in Port of Spain, Trinidad, in 1926. Her exotic good looks can be attributed to the rich mix of her ancestry. Her father, Henry, was Indian, and her mother, Ruth, a mixture of Trinidadian, Scottish, Irish, and Venezuelan.

Mona was born in a poor part of Port of Spain, but Henry was an accountant and Ruth a determined woman with a keen business brain. The family soon worked their way up the social ladder and found themselves living in the select area of St Clair.

Ruth and Henry had five daughters, all of whom went to the prestigious St Joseph's Convent School. Henry had a drink problem, which meant Ruth ruled the roost, often collecting her husband's salary on payday before he could waste it on drink.

It soon became obvious that Mona had a beautiful singing voice, and in typical Ruth style, she took her to the local radio station and proudly announced that, "My daughter sings." Sure enough, the radio station was impressed enough to give teenage Mona a weekly slot.

Trinidad became very "Americanized" during World War II, and Mona was exposed to and adored the voices of singers like Ella Fitzgerald and Lena Horne.

In 1948, she made the decision to leave Trinidad, but surprisingly her destination was not New York, but London, England.

She sailed, first class, on the famous ship the *Empire Windrush*, which is celebrated for bringing the first batch of West Indian immigrants to Britain. There were ships and immigrants long before the *Windrush*, but the name has become synonymous with the influx of West Indians who helped rebuild Britain after the ravages of World War II.

Mona is recorded on the passenger list as a clerk, but her fame was such that the *Daily Mirror* reported that, "On board the *Windrush* was the blues singer and saxophonist Mona Baptiste." This was accompanied by what has become an iconic photograph of Mona, saxophone at her lips, being watched over by several West Indian RAF members who had travelled with her on the *Windrush*. As Liam will tell you, Mona could not play the saxophone!

It certainly didn't take long for Mona's singing talent to be recognized as, within six weeks of her arrival, she was appearing on BBC radio along with Stanley Black and his Dance Orchestra and her fellow *Windrush* passenger, the calypsonian Lord Beginner.

Appearances flowed after that, and in March 1949, the *Musical Express* described Mona as "the new singing discovery," who had signed to sing with Cab Kaye and his Cabinettes. After one show in Birmingham, the press reported that, "The best part of the show had nothing to do with jazz or bebop. [It was] Cab Kaye's vocal duet with lovely Jamaican [sic] Mona Baptiste." This mistake of calling Mona "Jamaican" was not an isolated error. The British press, even nowadays, often suggests all the immigrants on the *Windrush* were from Jamaica.

Mona toured the country with Cab Kaye and his band building up her reputation as a top class singer.

She didn't work exclusively with Kaye and also became a member of the Stéphane Grappelli Quintet. Grappelli was a world famous jazz violinist who became a life-long friend of Mona's.

It was while working with Grappelli that Mona got the breakthrough that led her to become a star right across Europe.

Warner Brothers had identified a young French singer and entertainer called Yves Montand as their next "big thing". He was touted as the next Danny Kaye. Originally spotted by Edith Piaf, Montand had become a famous face in France, but Warner Brothers wanted to extend his popularity beyond his home country.

In the summer of 1949, Bernard Delfont (later Baron Delfont) the British-based impresario created a show at the Saville Theatre in London to exhibit Montand's many talents.

Partly in order to maintain a Gallic theme, the Stéphane Grappelli Quintet was recruited as part of the extravaganza. Montand must have been pleasantly surprised when he found that Grappelli's beautiful black singer could speak fluent French. He was so impressed with Mona's voice that he invited her to perform in Paris. She did so, was a huge success and her fame rocketed.

Press reports claim that Mona could speak eight different languages, although Liam feels this may be an exaggeration. She was certainly fluent in Spanish and German, as well, of course, as French and English.

When Mona first met Liam at Baden-Baden, she was keen to learn some Irish. A good place to start might be how to say "hello" in Irish. Mona was taught that this was "pog mo thoin". This appealed to the rather juvenile sense of humour of the Irish delegation, as the words actually mean "kiss my a———". It didn't take Mona long to latch onto the joke, but she regularly played on it at the conference and in later years by pretending she really did think it meant hello.

It was during Mona's time with the Yves Montand show that she made her first TV appearance in a programme called *Coloured Follies*.

Immediately after the Yves Montand show ended and before appearing on the continent, Mona extended her repertoire into lavish musical productions such as *Panama* and *Montmartre*, with a cast of over forty. A review of Montmartre in November 1949 said that, "Vocal honours go chiefly to Mona Baptiste, whose treatment of well-chosen songs, plus a pleasing stage presence, marks a commendable performance."

Elsewhere she had been described as "the sepia angel of song" and "the sensational vocalist Mona Baptiste".

Mona made the transition from musical extravaganzas to her first pure acting role in June 1951 when she appeared in London in the play *Tiger Bay*. She was described as the "coffee-hued song girl".

Mona was a huge success in Paris, and this led to appearances throughout Europe, particularly in Germany. In the early 1950s, she took up residence in Hamburg.

Between July 1954 and January 1956, Mona had four chart hits in Germany, three of which got into the top ten. Her greatest hit was "Es Liegt Was In Der Luft" (There's Something in the Air), which reached number two and spent twenty-eight weeks in the top ten.

An effort to launch Mona's career in the United States in 1956/57 didn't quite come off. But it did lead to the American *Billboard* magazine of 15 December 1956 reviewing her single, "It's Been A Long, Long Time", in language that reads strangely to us in modern times: "a sultry new Deutsche Gramaphon [Mona's record label] chick makes her bow in a style that's bound to have its impact. The thrush sings this standard World War Two tune in a slow, sexy way that will make [disc] jockeys and audiences sit bolt upright."

Mona was in demand throughout Europe. In April 1957, she sang in three different countries, in three languages, over a period of three days. She sang a French song on Belgian TV and then travelled to London to sing on *The Ted Ray Show*, followed by an appearance on German TV the next day. She was reported to be "now established as one of the highest paid stage artistes in Germany".

She appeared in many films in Germany, the most popular being *Symphonie in Gold* in 1956.

She continued to perform in Britain, where she had a weekly radio programme and appeared along with the likes of Cliff Richard on the popular music programme *Oh Boy*.

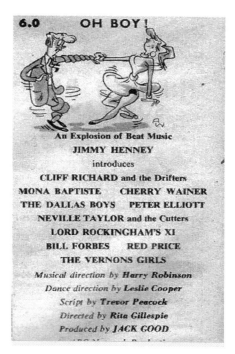

There is a lot of misinformation about Mona on the internet, including the year of her birth (it was 1926, not 1928) and her place of death (Dublin, not Krefeld in Germany). It is also suggested that Mona retired from the entertainment industry in the late 1950s. Nothing could be further from the truth, as Liam can testify from Mona's regular trips to perform in Germany. Indeed, she was performing in Germany only a few weeks before her sudden death in June 1993.

The main difference in Mona's life following her marriage to Liam was that she was now Mrs Morrison and happy and proud to be so. She had no airs and graces and was as much at ease doing housework as she was singing in front of an audience. She still loved performing just as much as she had when she was a child star in Trinidad, but now she could choose where and when she wanted to perform.

When Mona was not performing, she loved to stay at home to cook and bake. As another reminder of Trinidad, she would buy fresh fish, crabs, and lobster from the fishermen at Bulloch Harbour, about eight miles away at Dalkey in south Dublin Bay. What should accompany the freshly prepared fish was subject to a definite clash of cultures. For Mona, no meal was complete without rice. But Liam, an Irishman through and through, preferred potatoes. To avoid any diplomatic incidents Mona usually provided both rice and potatoes.

Mona's "jet-setting" did have its advantages though. In 1973, Mona was providing the entertainment on a cruise ship destined for Brazil. Liam was able to join her on the four-week cruise, although he had to use a little "poetic licence" in convincing his boss that he would only be away for two weeks when, in fact, his staff had agreed to secretly cover for him for all four weeks.

They say absence makes the heart grow fonder, and that was true for Mona and Liam, who cherished their time together in Ireland, where Mona was very much Mrs Morrison. She never lost her "identity" though, and to this day, twenty-seven years since her death, her name is still displayed proudly alongside Liam's on the front door of their home.

Bill Hern

CHAPTER 9

REFLECTIONS

In the seventies, I was asked to brief a young local actor and playwright on his first trip to America as part of a two-week multicity cultural programme known as the Irish Fortnight under the aegis of Dr Eoin McKiernan of the Irish American Cultural Institute. He was very keen to conquer the new world, and I had concerns that his enthusiasm, without due preparation and planning, might end badly. I tried to dissuade him and encouraged him to make contacts and plans so as to avoid disappointments.

Many years later, I encountered him on a Dublin street and reintroduced myself. With a wee hint of mischief, I asked him how his American trip had worked out. He proceeded to tell me modestly, before I interrupted him. I had indeed followed his progress over the intervening years and had noted his several successful film. Among them were the Oscar-winning *My Left Foot*; *In the Name of the Father*; and, based on his own story, *In America*. Indeed, that young man turned out to be playwright, screenwriter, and filmmaker Jim Sheridan. Not all my judgements were flawless.

***

For the first fifty years of my life, Ireland was a nation that lived with emigration. And for the following thirty years, the trend was reversed. We became a land welcoming immigrants to enrich the living experience of the population. I'll share a few vignettes I observed as an illustration of the changing street scene, which would pass by the attention of those under forty years of age as nothing to remark on:

- A smartly dressed young businesswoman gives a local " knight of the road" a cup of coffee as he sits on the pavement. Nothing unusual here, except she was a lady of colour, not Irish-born, giving a handout to an Irish-born down on his luck.

- A father leads two six-year-old girls by the hand, on one on each side, to school—one a pale-skinned red-haired child and the other of dark complexion and hair in cornrows, an obvious happy family scene.

- And yet another example of the seamless integration of the new Irish into current life, a young Asian youth helps a poorly sighted local pensioner across a busy street crossing.

Indeed, we have come a long and positive way.

Reasons to be grateful

Among my many reasons to be grateful are:

- The blessing of a happy home life, good parents and siblings, and cousins at home and abroad in Britain and North America

- The lasting friendships of boyhood pals, especially Johnny Woods

- Good health and good neighbours

- The love of the Irish language and my Gaeltacht friends in Baile an Fheirtéaraigh Co Chíarraí— Ballyferriter Co. Kerry

- Making the acquaintance, through my work, of writers Maeve Binchy and Nuala O'Faolain, later to become my friends, and of Tipperary stage and film set designer Seán Kenny, who, in 1950, sailed the Atlantic from Dublin to New York in a gaff-rigged yacht the *Ituna* with three companions before continuing his architectural and artistic career.

And so to Good Friday 2020 and the lockdown due to the Covid-19 pandemic and three months of being confined to barracks with strict conditions for the over seventy brigade. Without being too disrespectful, it gave new meaning to the agony in the garden.

But hope springs eternal. And bilingual is the motto and inspiration as displayed on the frontage of my local watering hole, Charlie Chawke's Searsons Pub Restaurant, hoping to be back in business shortly:

Naisiún Taghta le Chéile trí Fanacht ar Shiuil óna Chéile

Fan Slán, Fan Folláin, Éirimis Arís.

One nation coming together by staying apart. Stay safe, stay well. We will rise again.

Three Swallow Dives from the ten metre diving platform
Billy Morrison – Valy Demery – Eddie Heron

Sandycove Diving Team at Blackrock Baths

L to R Billy Morrison Val Demery Eddie Heron Dano
O'Brien Jerry Daly Seated Joe Keegan Eddy Cody

Author

**Author's Father
Tom Morrison**

**Handstand dive from ten metre diving
platform, Blackrock Baths.**

The author at three or four years of age with sisters, Jane on left and Mary on right.

Mona Baptiste

I've climbed
God's mountain

A door will open
Anyone can find
their own door
It takes a lot of courage to ask
Take time & ask

Donal Walsh

85TH YEAR.   NO. 4399.   (NEW NO. 1723)

A Catholic chaplain, Fr. M. C. Morrison, of Dublin, and a Jewish chaplain, the Rev. L. H. Hardman, of Leeds, each say their own prayers for the dead over the communal grave of some of the victims of Belsen concentration camp.

Polish priest might say

REQUIEM FOR NAZI

Mohammedan Envoy May go to Vatican

THE Egyptian Foreign Minister is considering the appointment of the first Mohammedan

Printed in France by Amazon
Brétigny-sur-Orge, FR

12352376R10064